NEW BEGINNINGS

RHYTHMIC PUBLISHERS

Contents

Rhythmic Publishers   *v*

Disclaimer   *vii*

Acknowledgements   *ix*

About the Book   *xi*

1. No Man's Land   1

2. The Midnight Mystery   3

3. Missed Reunion   6

4. Under The Changing Sky   10

5. A Crow Named Black   19

6. A Ray Of Hope   30

7. To Believe Or Not To Believe   34

Author Details

8. Sanchita Chakraborty   49

9. Dr Debosree Ghosh   50

10. Mala Bhattacharya   52

11. Mandira Ghosh   54

12. Dr Debasri Mukherjee   56

13. Dr Sukanya Bhattacharya   58

14. Aishi Bandyopadhyay   60

Rhythmic Publishers

-Seeking harmony through words.

We, at *Rhythmic Publishers*, believe in the power of words as a means of seeking harmony in a chaotic universe. We are eager to provide aspiring writers with a premium platform to express themselves. Attractive packages are available for both solo books and anthologies (editorial services and book design included). We work diligently to make a book the best version of itself and client satisfaction is our top priority.

Contact us on:

Instagram: @rhythmicpublishers

E-mail: rhythmicpublications23@gmail.com

We are also on **Twitter** and **LinkedIn**

Disclaimer

This anthology is a collection of poems, stories and write-ups written by talented writers from various parts of the country.

We have guided them not to use any copyrighted content and done our best to check plagiarism.

If any copyrighted content is detected, neither the publisher, nor the compiler nor the editor will be responsible in any way. Co-authors will be responsible for their own content.

All rights reserved. No part of this book may be reproduced, stored in a retrieval system, or transmitted, in any form by any means, electronic, mechanical, magnetic, optical, chemical, manual, photocopying, recording or otherwise, without the prior written consent of its Compiler.

Compiler and Editor: Aishi Bandyopadhyay

Book Layout and Cover Design: Romit Majumder

Acknowledgements

Rhythmic Publishers expresses its gratitude towards the extremely talented co-authors, who have enthusiastically contributed their write-ups for this book.

About The Book

New Beginnings is a collection of literary works. The assortment of stories and poems in this anthology are as profoundly meaningful as they are entertaining. Some pieces are a commentary on the human situation and society at large, whereas others serve to amuse and delight as the readers' imagination takes flight. All in all, *New Beginnings* offers the readers a perfect balance of realism and artistry, so much so, that there is never a dull moment.

1
No Man's Land

Sanchita Chakraborty

At the edge of twilight, I stand, I pause.
The night fades, yet no dawn calls my name.
A step forward leads to a storm,
A step back feels empty.

I cannot bear the dull past,
But I cannot embrace the daring future.
I am stuck in the "in-between".

I find myself in the realm of uncertainty,
In the state of nothingness, trapped in fear,
Wandering through a land of limbo,
Suspended between two states, unable to move,
I stand in the hush of endless sorrow,
Belonging to neither,
Yet affected by both!

However, the river won't rest, the winds won't still, and
time won't pause.
So I gather my breath,
Not waiting for the light, but learning to glow.
Not bound by echoes, not lost in haze,
I step beyond – into my own space.

ᑭᑭᑭ

2

The Midnight Mystery

Dr Debosree Ghosh

It was a stormy summer night in Kolkata, the kind that brought a welcome drop in temperature and a sense of relief to the sweltering city. The rain poured down, drumming against the windows and roofs, as the thunder growled and boomed in the distance. The streets were empty. There were only occasional flashes of lightning that illuminated the dark sky.

As the clock struck 2:00 AM, the city slumbered, wrapped in a cocoon of silence. But, I was wide awake, hunched over my desk, racing against time to finish some urgent academic assignments from the college. The rain created a soothing melody that helped me focus, and I worked steadily, fuelled by a glass of chilled coke.

As I finished my tasks and glanced at the clock, I felt a sense of satisfaction wash over me. It was 2:30 AM, and the storm showed no signs of abating. I took a sip of water, feeling the cool liquid slide down my throat, and then decided to take a peek outside.

I pushed aside the curtain and gazed out into the darkness. The streetlights were out, plunging the street into an inky blackness. The only sound was the relentless patter of the rain and the occasional rumble of thunder. I felt a shiver run down my spine as I stood there, lost in the eerie beauty of the stormy night.

Just as I was about to turn away, I heard it. The calling bell rang outside, shrill and insistent, cutting through the silence like a knife. I froze, my heart skipping a beat as I wondered who could be visiting at such an ungodly hour.

The bell rang again, and I had a strange feeling of mixed anxiety, curiosity and fear. I checked the time, wondering if I was dreaming, but the clock confirmed that it was indeed 2:30 AM. I thought about all the possible explanations – a neighbour in distress, a friend or family member in need of help – but none of them seemed plausible as any of them would have called up my number.

The bell stopped ringing, and I was left standing there, my mind racing with questions. Had I imagined the whole thing? Was it some kind of prank? I decided to investigate further and peered out of the window, searching for any sign of movement. But there was none. The street was empty, the only sound was of the rain and thunder. I felt a shiver run down my spine as I realized that I was the only one awake in the darkness, experiencing an uncanny event.

The bell rang again, and I knew then that I had to do something. I decided to check the door, to see if anyone was standing there, waiting for me to answer it. I approached the door cautiously, my heart pounding in my chest, and peered through the eyehole.

But there was no one there. The bell had stopped ringing, and an eerie silence had fallen over the apartment. I felt a sense of unease wash over me as I realized that I was facing a mystery that seemed impossible to solve.

It wasn't until I decided to Google the phenomenon that the mystery was finally resolved. It turned out that the stormy weather had caused an electrical interference that had triggered the doorbell. These voltage surges, mediated by lightning strike, sometimes trigger a doorbell chime to activate. So a doorbell may start ringing even if no one is physically present near it and pressing the button. Such electrical fluctuations act like "phantom" signals and are simply caused by lightning strikes and voltage surges in the power lines.

As I read the explanation, I felt a sense of relief wash over me. It wasn't a ghost or a prankster – it was just science. I smiled to myself, feeling a sense of wonder at the strange and mysterious ways of the world. And as I drifted off to sleep, lulled by the sound of the rain, I knew that I would never forget this strange and mysterious stormy night.

ᗐᗐᗐ

3
Missed Reunion

Mala Bhattacharya

This poem is based on a "missed reunion" of school friends. As the years pass by, school friends tend to slowly drift apart and lose contact with each other. Remarkably, however, we have kept up our friendship since we passed out ICSE in 1975. We've had a couple of reunions before, but this third one was very deeply meaningful to all of us, especially in the light of the passing away of a dear friend to Cancer, last year. As this get-together was so special, there sometimes develops a misconception that those who missed it (unfortunately, like myself) could have tried harder to make it. Hence this poem...

Please try and understand that this Reunion
Was also special to me ---

For it would bring together
A bunch of loved faces nearer to me!

I would have loved to revisit
Those carefree days spent long gone by.

Where innocuous laughter, gaiety and fun
Were more than reasons to cry.

Especially, when the responsibilities of adulthood;
decision-making
Was a distant thing...

Who would have known then, that the very thought of a
reunion
Would throb our very being??

So Girls, on behalf of all those who missed this soul-stirring
meet...
Know that our reasons of not attending run very very
deep!

So every time you remind us, what we have really missed...
Believe you me, none Know better than us...what we
have really missed!

Life is a journey, with each passing day we realize,
...of Happy laughter, painful phases and a lot of
goodbyes!

Personal goals met, targets achieved...

Feted with awards, accolades received,
Loved ones were fine, worries were at bay...

Emotions were validated
Prompt and sans delay.

If you were one of them
Then you are lucky, I must say,
Do thank God sincerely, for having a fortunate year!

'Coz there are many who have had moments of fear,
Of a loved one's frail health...
Of the knowing that the END is NEAR..!

So the ups and downs went on as it does every year...
Probably, this year too had a tad more downs than ups
to bear...

Yet in the midst of it all
Hope never left us,
Blessings were counted
...and gratitude towards all.

As we look forward to another New Year...
May God shower His blessings to all our dears
Keep them safe and sound and forever near!

Happy, healthy and prosperous for sure,
That's all we can pray, for and to ensure!!
ᕤᕤᕤ

RHYTHMIC PUBLISHERS

4
Under the Changing Sky

Mandira Ghosh

It's past midnight. I have just completed my work hours. I check the clock—it is 2:05 a.m.—and I shut down my laptop. Working the night shift is pretty exhausting. Tiredness can reach your nerves sometimes. And when it's the first day of the week, it seems more difficult. But after a long hour of screen exposure, your eyes also refuse to sleep. So, instead of reaching towards the bed, I choose to wrap up and organize my room as well as myself for a good reading session.

Recently, I started reading *Walden* by Henry David Thoreau.

After wrapping up everything, I am just about to light the Himalayan dusk fragranced candle, which I recently started obsessing with, when I hear that it's raining outside. It's mid-December- winter and the rain. Making the wildest combination to pause and fill my mind with nothing but void. I choose to sit by the window. The sound of the rain feels quite therapeutic. I don't know how much time I have lost, only listening to the rain. I got my senses back when the clock struck three. Maybe, I half-slept for a while.

By now, there is no sound of rain anymore. So, I feel like going to my balcony. It's pleasantly cold. The sky has cleared up very fast. Stars are visible again. The western sky looks divine. I realize that there will be a full moon in a matter of days.

Nature is so unpredictable. Just a few minutes back, there was no sign of the moon and stars and it was raining quite well. Now it's all clear and bright. Life is also like that; it is so unpredictable that you never know what the next moment holds for you.

For the past couple of days, the weather has been erratic. It's raining unpredictably. Like yesterday, for example. It was my day off. Since I hadn't made any plans for the day, after lunch, I decided to go to the library, where I picked up the book, *Walden.* When I was about to take my leave, I realized that it was dull outside and clouds had suddenly covered up the sun. It started to rain. It was the weekend, so, the library was filled with many book lovers. One of them was preparing to exit at the same time I was and also got stuck because of the rain.

Institutes and situations conspire to weave life together, referred to as coincidence. I am a believer in serendipity. Rain was the icebreaker here.

I know most of the regular visitors at the library. But this person was unfamiliar to me. It's not like I spend all my free time at the library, but I visit the library from time to time. But, yes, he was actually new to the library; it was only last week that he had started coming. He introduced himself as Vihaan. He is a banker and an influencer. We vibed over coffee and agreed to go to the newly opened café nearby.

I never drop a chance to have coffee. In addition to that, I like knowing people's stories and their perspectives. Here I am, an educator and introvert, who expresses as well as hides herself behind written words. On the other hand, Vihaan is a banker and an influencer who portrays himself in front of a camera every day. The perspectives will be unique. And indeed it was.

Before leaving, I went to sign the register, which he had already done. Nevertheless, he followed me there.

"Niharika, what a beautiful name," he remarked.

I realized that I hadn't introduced myself yet. "Sorry, I forgot to introduce myself," I said with a smile.

He smiled back to say it's fine.

We paved our way towards the newly opened café, just two buildings apart from the library. It was raining quite well, so we took our steps carefully and reached the place walking along the available shades. The café was quite pretty and cosy and the lighting was eye-soothing. The best part of the café was its glass window walls. Raindrops trickled down them. The outside was getting dimmer with time. We took a seat near one of the windows. We both ordered plain black coffee. And our conversation began to unfold.

I told him about my career as a Maths teacher, how I started from a small room and am now teaching worldwide. Besides being a blogger, I do write a little here and there. Overjoyed, he expressed how he had also studied Maths, did his MBA, and is now working in the World Bank.

So far, with the coffee and the Maths, the conversation was going on similarities until he noticed the book that I had issued from the library: *Walden*. After that, our conversation opened up new horizons.

"Oh wow, you like to read classics?"

"Areh, no, once in a while, I just throw myself into classics to explore a little about what has been praised by people over the decade," I said.

"Okay, still, it's pretty awesome."

I smiled and asked, "Tell me, what kind of books do you read?"

"I read autobiographies and mostly non-fiction books. I feel that they add a lot of value to life. I even made videos about how reading and applying the lifestyle of successful people helped me to gain a lot of stability and a little success. Do you read these books?"

"Wow, that's really wonderful. I rarely read non-fiction.

Maybe watching your videos can give me some insights." I smiled a little hesitantly.

"But *Walden* is a non-fiction, right?"

"Yes, sometimes I surrender myself to these books and finish them too. I wanted to read *Walden* for so long, but now I am just getting into it. However, I love to read fiction more. I know people think that fiction is only for entertainment; they are indeed, but, it also adds value to our emotions and our thinking, in the most unexpected ways. That's the beauty of fiction. You never start reading it seriously, but it might change something within you without your awareness. That's just my view." I smiled to make the whole conversation less intense.

He reciprocated my smile and said, "That's quite an impressive view indeed."

He paused and asked, "Don't you think knowing about others' lives through autobiographies can show you the paths that you need to follow? Maybe guide you and help you to make decisions more firmly?"

"I do find it delightful to know about other people's lives—their struggles, their views about things- but, it is just limited to that. I don't want to reach the success they had reached by following in their footsteps. Everyone is different; their lives are also different. I might not be successful like them, but, that will just be my experience. We humans are here to add our verses only. Sorry, inspired by *Dead Poets Society*." I smiled and held my hands up in a gesture of surrender.

He gave me a big smile in surprise and acknowledgment. A little silence befell us while we both took a sip of our coffee.

He was the one who spoke first, "Hey, your watch is beautiful. The blue colour makes it very charming. I can see your bag and your mobile cover; all are shades of blue. Any specific reason for this obsession with blue?"

I smiled and put down my cup. "I love the colour blue. Someone told me that blue represents death. But, I feel that it depicts frozenness. Something beyond what we can feel. A life beyond the outer shell. It's much deeper than our senses. It's cool, calm, and composed, yet solid, structured, and profound." I glanced at his watch. "Your leather-coloured watch looks classy, though. Does it mean anything to you?"

"Yes, as you said, it's classy and a little authoritative. But in a submissive manner."

We met for the very first time and were having our very first coffee. Our exchange of words was taking place perfectly, like the correct parts of a jigsaw puzzle. The rain was getting heavier, asking for our attention. It was much darker outside by that time. The street lights illuminated the raindrops on the glass. Vihaan seemed calm while looking outside; but his eyes had a spark to them. His neatly shaved beard and well-organized, short hair made him look sharper. Our silence was filled with the sound of raindrops. He was staring at me, and as our eyes met, I smiled and looked back at the window. His gaze was fixed at me for a few moments. I could feel that. Then he picked up his cup to take another sip of the coffee.

I broke the silence after a while, "How would you like to define yourself if it would be a one-or-two-line verse on you?"

He looked at me; his gaze turned misty. He broke the eye contact and said, "An outgoing person, a workaholic, a little disciplined. Loves challenges to get to the best version of himself."

The silence continued.

"If I asked you the same question? What would be your verse?"

I looked at him for a few seconds. He did the same. The eyes spoke their own silent language. "An introverted person who sometimes puts herself out and loves to know people and their stories, but then she needs her own time to fall back and refill. And a person who hides herself behind words."

We kept staring into each other's eyes for some time.

I shifted my glance towards my coffee and took another sip. He followed my action.

I said, "See, now the whole world is watching videos, and there are writers also who come up with their poetry, and stories and present them through videos. Still, I am hiding behind words, writing blogs, and expressing myself, still not confident enough to come in front of the camera.

Maybe one day I'll make the videos and post them too, but, today is not that day. Maybe I can get inspired by other writers who are making their videos, and by following in their footsteps, I'll be able to reach heights I never thought about, but that won't be organic for me, neither do I want to do it now, nor am I ready to be that person yet.

You know, as an introvert, I face the faces of people with the question— 'Why couldn't I be more social? What is it that is eating me or depressing me so much?' Sometimes, it is difficult to explain, but I do socialize, and I feel happy about it. However, after that, I just need a bit of time with myself to be clearer with my thoughts. I've just accepted myself like that."

"Have you ever considered pushing boundaries and getting out of your comfort zone? You know, by following strict discipline, people changed their lives and themselves also. Have you ever considered what will happen if you don't fall back and keep showing up continuously?"

"Yes, I have. I often put myself in situations and works that cause me discomfort. And none of them have made me feel regret. But it is just my thing to have my own time. After that, I'm usually more present and productive mentally. And 'me-times' give me clarity of thought, solace, and a feeling of contentment. And why should I change myself into a person I don't want to be? Life is more than that; it unfolds in its own way. We also unfold with time- our desires and thoughts change over time. Life surprises us in its unpredictable manner. Why should we be like someone else, when we can perfectly be us? If the greatest artists had thought of following a rule, would the classics have been created?

Why not pause, once in a while, to be in the moment and cherish it? Life will change its track, resembling the weather. See, it's not raining anymore. But, meanwhile, an unexpected encounter unfolds." I smiled.

He looked towards the window and smiled. "Yes, the pause seems to end too fast."
I smiled. "By the way, which book did you issue?"

"It's *My Autobiography*, the autobiography of Charlie Chaplin."

"Oh, wow, I would also love to read that book one day. That will be on my to-do list from now on."

I insisted on paying the bill. But we agreed on splitting it.

I got so lost in my thoughts that I didn't know when I had lost track of the moon. The western sky seems lonely now. And a little beam of light from the eastern sky brought me back into consciousness.

I check the time; it's 5:45 AM. I am going to have a long day today. Before I embark on it, I need at least three to four hours of sleep.

ᐅᐅᐅ

5

A Crow Named Black

Dr Debasri Mukherjee

Aww! Sweet! That is my boy. Kill. Kill. Kill...No, no, no... it is pecking his eyes out... ! Yes! Grabbed it by the neck. Now one snap and the head's off rainbow neck plumage an' all. I think it's time to land on the nearest branch. A few of my brothers might be on the lookout too. Best to be the first off the block! I dip down, circling the topmost branches, looking for a sturdier lower branch to land on while keeping one wary eye on the prey, or, to be honest, on the severed head of the prey which the dog has very obligingly thrown aside while starting on the body.

There! A likely-looking branch. I land, silent as a shadow. I have always prided myself on my landings. Even when I was an ugly, cawing, irritating little chick learning to fly at my mother's insistence (accompanied by a lot of hard painful pecking, by the way), my landings were my specialty. My brothers and sisters made fools of themselves trying to land on their feet after their first attempts at flying, but I, I was sublime. I may not have been able to stay afloat for more than a few minutes, but, I always landed on my two feet. And always silently. Nary a twig or leaf was disturbed when I landed. My mother was so proud. She showed me off to her friends, puffing her dark chest in pride every time I executed a perfect landing. Boy, was everybody jealous! I remember our neighbour, the crow-pheasant. A big beast of a bird as she seemed to me then. Her chicks weren't much older than I but were more well-built and had strong brown wings. You should have seen the way the mother cavaliered them through the day trying to make them learn to land like me. Oh, the antics they pulled... I would be hoarse with laughter at their desperate attempts to outshine me. I was the king of the block. No one, not even the kites or the occasional hawk that visited our tree, could outdo me in executing the perfect landing. Those were happy days.

A sudden movement on the left of my peripheral vision jerks me out of my happy musings of bygone days. Oh no! It's a kite. He has seen my prize too and has just landed on the topmost branch of the adjoining tree, and is biding his time. If it came down to a race for the peacock head, I know I don't stand a chance. The kite's young and healthy, a lot stronger, and faster than I am. I'll be hardly off the block before he is off with the head. I must think fast. He may be faster and stronger than me, but he's also dumber. He'll never make his move before the dog finishes his meal and saunters away because that's the rule of the jungle. You respect those stronger and higher than you in the hierarchy, or you pay the price. I was never one for rules anyway.

I decide fast. Desperate times require desperate measures. And besides, the harder and more dangerous the game, the sweeter the reward. I glance once at the kite, gauging its distance from the target. If I take it by surprise, I might just gain those crucial few seconds I need to reach the finishing line first. Alright then, here goes nothing. I give a muffled caw to draw the kite's attention, spread my wings, and dive. Straight towards the peacock carcass. High above myself, I can hear the kite spreading its wings to follow. My subterfuge seems to have worked. I fly as fast as I can, but can feel him gaining on me. Below, the half-eaten peacock carcass and the feeding dog are coming nearer and nearer. Now I feel a faint pull down my slipstream, the kite is at my heels. I'm almost eye-to-eye with the dog. I'll barge right into him. Focus! A sharp twist of the left wing. A tearing pain through my side as I turn against the wind pressure without slowing down. I almost hit the ground as I stretch my feet to grab the head. With a burst of speed, I'm rising again. Faster than I've ever flown in my life. Through the screaming air in my ears, I hear the screech and growl as the kite barges into the dog. That would have been an encounter worth watching. But by now I'm high above the trees, their canopy hiding everything on the ground. Not that I'm much concerned. I have my prize. This'll be the best meal I've had in three months. So, presently, I don't care if the world breaks apart, so long as it does so after my meal. Oh, sweet life! I can't wait.

I circle above the roofs of the buildings looking for a potential landing spot. It must be a secluded spot or else I'll not know a moment's peace. My fellow crows may not be very visionary in exerting themselves to improve their lot, but if someone among them by some lucky chance, or a lot of effort like I put in today, does manage something good, the others seem to feel entitled to a share, just by virtue of being from the same species and social order. Bunch of crap, I say. I earned this prize and I'll enjoy it in solitude. I see a prospective tin shade and head towards it. It is late afternoon and the sun is on its return journey, it's a day's work done. The soft slanting rays reflect off the jungle of concrete rooftops. A decade-old memory fleetingly passes before my eyes. I'm flying high in the sky, looking down at a dark green stretch interspersed with a few rooftops. My vision clears and the present looms up before my searching eyes. An impersonal grey mass interspersed by a few lone green trees, the last remaining survivors. It fills me with a strange sadness as I circle down. Like a well drying up. Like a living body decaying part by interminable part. I've never been anywhere other than this city in my fifteen years of life, yet, I learn about the world beyond from my migrating friends. Every year they come with new terrifying stories of dead seas, burnt forests, molten glaciers, and barren lands. So many of them are vanishing. Each time I see fewer of them. I don't know where the missing ones have gone. I never get a straight answer from the ones that do arrive. It is as if they fear even thinking about it. I don't pester them. I hate those who prod and pry.

I land safely on my tin shade and skip to a comfortable spot. It is not easy while holding the head in my talons, but I manage well enough. I let go of the head finally and settle myself down to enjoy my hard-earned feast. Bang! The sound is like a gunshot startling me so badly that I almost fall off the shade. Correcting my position, I peer upwards. No, it's not a gunshot. From what I can see, it's a door banging off the wall. Oh bother! That is a human woman coming this way. She has the entire roof to herself and she chooses to head my way. How bad can one's luck get? I consider ignoring her and continuing with my meal, but even I, who risks getting eaten by a big bad dog, am wary of humans. That is because these two-legged creatures do not exhibit any rational behaviour at all. A dog, or any other creature for that matter, you can trust to behave in a certain predictable pattern. If you are a prey, your predator will attack you when they are hungry or leave you alone. I have taught myself to recognize signs of aggression in all the other creatures with whom I co-exist. But not humans. You can never tell what they'll do or why. They don't eat us, yet for no apparent reason, they often try to hurt us. We could have lived with that and adjusted ourselves accordingly if that was the established behaviour of their species against ours. But it's not. There is this whole other bunch of them who try to be so sweet and feed and shelter us. And there are still others who ignore us completely. We are left totally confused. How do you behave with creatures who are perpetually unsure as to how to live in harmony with the other occupants of their planet? That is why I'm wary of this approaching woman. I do not know which faction she belongs to.

She is coming too close for comfort. I give an irritated caw and take off from the shade, leaving behind the peacock head, praying it won't be noticed. As the woman walks towards the edge of the roof, I circle above her head, hoping desperately that she will leave soon. She has reached the edge. I think she is talking but I don't see anyone else around. That is another strange thing about these humans. We crows are talkative creatures. We are always conversing, or rather, arguing amongst ourselves about something or the other, never coming to a consensus. But that is not really the point of the exercise. We talk to hear each other's voices. To remind ourselves that we are not alone. But I see these humans often in cheerful conversation with empty space. They have built these big machines to help them do what we do with our talons and eyes and wings and beaks. But they seem to have forgotten about each other. Each seems like an island. Existing all alone, with no connection with each other. That is why they are so unpredictable. You cannot predict what you might find on an unknown island.

The woman is leaning over the parapet. She seems to be looking at something keenly. Oh crap! She has seen the peacock's head. I don't think she realizes what she is seeing. I see her leaning farther and farther down. Any further and she'll topple over. Not that I mind, but in that case, she'll dislodge my precious head. Oh my God! What is that horrible sound she just made? She must have realized what she was looking at finally because she shrunk back from the edge of the parapet as if struck by something. Now she's running back inside. Good. I'll just swoop down, pick up the head, and get out from here. Then I'll find some other safe place and devour my dinner. Just as I am thinking pleasurably of that last bit while extending my talons towards the colourful head, I hear the sound of running footsteps. Oh no! The female is back. And she has brought a male with her. I fly off again reluctantly. Now they are both staring at the peacock's head with eager and slightly repulsed interest. At least, that is what I think they are feeling from the expression on their faces. I keep circling overhead and wonder at the strange contradiction of these humans. If we feel revolted or repulsed by something, we will not stare at it with such interest but rather avoid it at all cost.

The humans are consulting about something. Now the man is walking off but not inside. He moves to the other side of the roof, seemingly searching for something. Oh, he has found it; a long wooden stick. He's walking with it towards the edge of the parapet again. What! No, no, no, no... You can't throw my prize away like that. I risked my life to get it. Noooo... he's pushing it off the parapet. I'll never find it again! No, no, no, no... I give a cry almost like a wail and dive to follow the peacock head down. Down...down...down... It's falling and I can't see where it's going through the shadows along the side of the building. But I follow anyway. I'll not give up that easily. It's mine and I will have it!

I land beside the door at the side of the building and slink in the shadows. It must have fallen somewhere around here. My eyesight isn't good in the dark, but I strain to see anyway, skipping here and there. But it's nowhere to be seen. The sun has gone down by now and heavy black shadows spread their silent wings, slowly engulfing the world around me. It's time to go home. All my friends and family are either already back home or on their way back, leaving the world to darkness and to me. Yet I refuse to leave. I search and search. A sharp cry reverberates in the silence around me. The owls are awake. An idea comes to me. Maybe, just maybe I might be able to find my prize again.

I hop out of the door's shadow and look up the nearest tree. The cry had come from somewhere up there. I spread my wings and fly towards the branches, hoping against hope that I'll find help there. As I near the sweeping branches of the banyan tree I can vaguely make out a white outline sitting on the branch nearest to me. I was right. The cry I had heard did come from this tree. I stop in mid-air before the faint white shape and approach with caution. When I'm near enough to be heard, I clear my throat and speak, "Hello Mr. Owl Sir. Your humble servant..." I wait for an answer. Then I try again. "Er... My name is Black, Sir. I am a crow. A black crow named Black..." No answer... I lose hope and am just about to turn back when I hear, "Isn't that a bit obvious?" I turn back towards the white owl but it's not he who has spoken. In the heavy darkness under the leaves and with my poor night vision, I had only managed to make out the shape of the white owl because of his colour. I had completely missed the tawny one sitting a few feet farther. "So? What do you have to say to that?" he asks again. "To what?" I enquire. "To the ridiculous situation where a black-coloured crow is called Black," he explains patiently. "Well, I suppose that is all my mother could come up with, seeing as she had to name seven squealing and cawing chicks who'd forget what they were called the moment they left the nest," I say. "Then how come you remember?" the tawny owl queries. "I don't really know," I muse, "perhaps that's because I have always been more aware of myself and my surroundings than any of my siblings." "Hmm. Well, that is what you say. But how do I know it's a real name and you didn't just invent it for my grandfather's benefit?" he asks, nodding towards the white owl who seems to be sleeping through the entire conversation. "Well, you don't know" is my rejoinder. "But since there is no one around to either confirm or deny my claim, I guess you'll just have to take my word for it." "You're pretty wise for a crow," he says. "Where'd you learn to speak like that?" "Well, I have a lot of friends who are not crows. They have travelled the world and tell me about the places they visited, the creatures they met, and the humans they came across. I have learnt to speak on varied topics because of them. Besides, I was born curious.”

The tawny owl looks across to me and seems to consider what I said. At least, that is what I suppose he is doing, since I can't really see him. My wings have started to ache badly from trying to keep myself upright and still in mid-air. I hope I can convince the owl to help me soon or I'll drop like a stone. “So, what was so pressing that you had to disturb my grandfather in his sleep, Black?” he asks. It is the opening I was looking for. “Oh, I'm in a bit of a fix,” I say. “You see, I risked my life to snatch a peacock head from the beaks of a kite and the jaws of a huge dog, only to have it thrown out, right before my eyes, by a human. It fell somewhere near that door down there and I can't see in the dark. I need your help to find it!” “Why should I bother to help you find a dead peacock head when you don't seem to have any intention of sharing it with me?”

“I'll share if you help me find it.” “Nah, I don't eat peacock.” “Then what do you want?”

He ponders awhile, then suddenly spreads his wings and flies towards me. I jump out of the way as he passes me with a whoosh of his wings, heading towards the door. “Come on. You want your head, or not?” He shouts back. Stunned, I follow sedately, not wanting to injure myself against the vaguely visible building walls. By the time I reach the said door, the tawny owl is nowhere to be seen. A shiver of fear passes through me. What if he finds the peacock head and takes it away? I'll never find him in the dark.

There is nothing I can do but wait and place my trust in

the goodwill of this stranger. I hear a shuffling noise from somewhere around the corner of the door and skip towards it. "Are you there?" I whisper into the darkness. No answer. "Hey? You there?" I ask again. Silence. I strain to see in the darkness. I can still hear shuffling. Whoa! I stumble back as the tawny owl suddenly appears before me. "What were you thinking? That I'll take your prize for myself?" There's a hint of laughter in his voice. I have the grace to look ashamed. "You know that is the problem with you crows. You don't trust anybody. We owls are proud. We hunt for our food. We don't steal it. Here, it got wedged in the hedge over there so took me a bit longer to find. Hope you enjoy it." He throws the peacock head near my feet.

I look at the pale shadow and then up at the owl. "Thank you. If you don't want to share it, then I don't know what to give you in return." "I'll hold you to it" he answers. "For now, just be thankful for a random act of kindness. They are few enough."

He spreads his wings and takes off. I stare at his dark form as it gets smaller. Midway up the tree, he stops and turns around. "By the way, my name's Jerome. You never asked," he shouts, then flies away. I am left staring at him, long after he's gone.

I finish my dinner at leisure and then decide to spend the night on the hedge around the corner where the peacock head had got stuck. The moon is out now, and the night is awash in an otherworldly hue. The creatures of the night make a cacophony of sounds. It's a soothing lullaby to my ears. The day's exertions have taken their toll. I fold my head into my wings and fall asleep to dreams of a beautiful peacock head with an owl's face. It's a weird dream and a fitting end to a weird day.

❧❧❧

6
A Ray of Hope

Dr Sukanya Bhattacharya

The inevitable happened.........I was grappling with the pain, the sudden loss. Completely devastated, finding it difficult to come to terms with it. My mother and I were more of friends, bonded for eternity. The love shared between us transcended time and space. I felt as if a part of myself was gone and it was something extremely difficult to reconcile with. The void, the emptiness seemed to engulf me with inexplicable horror. I fought with myself, became an avid reader of afterlife stories, hoping that time would heal the deep hurt inflicted upon her passing. I realized that her life was like summer flowers with their sweet fragrance, her death akin to the autumn leaf fall: sad but with a lingering fragrance of many precious memories to be etched indelibly in my heart.

As the days flew by, with me struggling to return back to the daily grind, regain normal composure and move forward with my usual fast-paced life, a little dumpling, barely three years old, quietly toed into my life. Little Samiya changed my world. The cute little cherub kept my world alive with all her innocence, verve, wit and antics. Samiya didn't step in alone. She was accompanied by her two older siblings, who also contributed to bring life back into the empty house. Very soon, the house was transformed into a home that it once had been when my mother waited for hours each day, anxiously, for my safe return. She would recline on a sofa and I would eagerly narrate each day's incident and we would then settle for late lunch and the conversation would go on and on with my sister intervening and adding some spice to the discussion. This was routine and I grew habituated to have lunch around 5:30PM, which is the normal tea time for most others. We would then go to Baba's room and mom used to give a news update of events taking place globally and in and around the neighbourhood. Baba loves Rabindrasangeet and each evening, my mother, my sister and I would congregate in the hallroom unplugging the music.

The house once again turned into a home, but this time, on a special note. The enormity of my anguish and gnawing loneliness now took a backseat. I tried to reconcile with the loss of my fulcrum of life. Since then, time has flown by in a quick flutter. The baby now goes to school with a huge embargo of books on her little back. I wonder why there is so much pressure on these young kids. Some reform is necessary I feel. One plus point I have noticed in Samiya is her unquenching thirst for knowledge. At times, she tries to imitate her class teacher and makes all in the house her students. She is undoubtedly a very hard task master, never to tolerate any nonsense from her pupils. You can expect to be hit by a stick which she brandishes quite menacingly, in case you are inattentive for a moment. Samiya loves to sing, recite poems and her dance poses are incredible. She is the apple of my eyes and extremely good at gymnastics. Her mother, a certified nurse, attends to my father, who is bedridden for the past eight years, following a failed hip joint surgery.

Samiya's immediate senior is her brother, Shan, who loves to fly kites and has a huge collection stacked in the corner of the house. The boy is super intelligent and loves computers. But of late, he is getting addicted to mobile games which I thoroughly disapprove of. I need to work out a strategy to deter him from pursuing this negative trait as this has impacted his studies adversely.

The eldest is her sister, Safia, a quiet, compassionate little girl who loves to dress well and flaunt fancy clothes. She is gifted with painting skills and has won accolades for her passion.

We were originally a close knit family of four, but, the number dropped to three with my mother's passing. We are now a regimen of seven, enough to make any visitor crazy. My parents didn't like to keep pets and we never had pets at home. The middle child is constantly pestering me to include a cute, cuddly pet dog in our house, promising to take full care of the animal. The other kids asked to get some caged parrots. My goodness gracious!! Are they conspiring to turn the house into a zoo? I am keeping my fingers crossed.

I have undertaken this mammoth responsibility of bringing up these three kids. My sister and I frequently have discussions about the future and occasionally rope in Baba to our conversation. The children, particularly Samiya, has become so much a part of our lives. If the older kids pay less attention to their curriculum, their mother reprimands them and swears to send them away to a boarding school to lead disciplined lives.

When the older kids go for their routine tuition classes, Samiya waits anxiously for them to return home. If they are late, she cannot hold back her tears. When I am back home from work, Samiya is the first to respond to the doorbell. She quickly clambers down the steps and stands on a stool to open the main door. Nobody is perhaps as delighted as Samiya when I am back home with a small bar of Cadbury's milk chocolate or a packet of Cadbury's gems. I feel there is a silver chord connecting all of us together and I hope and I pray that we can continue to live together like this for many years. The future / destiny will decide.

Maa, you are no longer with us physically, but, your memories linger on, imprinted in pixels, etched in our hearts.

ᐅᐅᐅ

7

To Believe or Not to Believe

Aishi Bandyopadhyay

It was 2 o' clock at night. Dipak sat up in bed with a start. It was freezing inside the room, despite the fact that all the doors and windows were closed. He pushed the blankets aside, got out of bed and tiptoed over to his roommate, who was fast asleep on the bed next to his.

'Joy,' he whispered.

Joy mumbled something and went back to sleep.

Dipak gave him a shove. 'Wake up you lazyhead!'

Joy sat up reluctantly and rubbed his eyes.

'Listen...listen to the sound of footsteps in the corridor outside our door,' said Dipak, in an anxious voice.

'Again? It's the third night in a row,' said Joy, as the two friends huddled close to each other and listened to the sound. Tap. Tap. Tap.

'I should go outside and check, just in case,' said Joy, getting out of bed.

'You *know* that we are the only two people in this house. There's not another living soul in the premises,' said Dipak.

'What if it's a trespasser?'

'We checked for trespassers on the first night. There was nobody there. Yet, the sounds kept coming.'

'You're right about that. So, what should we do now?'

'Don't go outside. It's too dangerous. Let morning come. We'll figure something out then.'

Dipak and Joy were both twenty-eight-year-olds. They were research scholars based in Kolkata who had come to Bankura for a week-long conference in Cultural Studies. All the other guest houses were occupied, and thus, the two had been given a place to stay in an old, isolated, bungalow-like house on the outskirts of the town. So far, however, their stay there was not going well. The uncanny sound of footsteps had kept them up the last two nights.

'I have my presentation tomorrow. If I don't get some sleep tonight I'm going to mess it up,' said Joy.

'You go to sleep. I'll stay on guard,' said Dipak.

'Thanks. I owe you one,' said Joy, as he climbed back into bed.

'This is nice,' said Joy, as he sat down on the field inside the campus after his presentation. Dipak and two other scholars- a boy and a girl- joined him. Arjun and Chandrani were born and brought up in Bankura and were now pursuing their PhD at a local university. They had been in a relationship for almost three years now.

Dipak yawned. 'I'm exhausted. I don't think I can manage to stay up for another night,' he said.

'What's this about staying up all night?' asked Chandrani.

Dipak and Joy exchanged meaningful glances with each other.

Dipak opened his mouth to say something but decided against it.

'Come on, you can tell us,' urged Arjun.

'Well...Here's the thing,' said Joy, as he embarked on his narrative.

Chandrani's eyes popped out of her head as she listened to the entire account.

'That old bungalow is haunted!' she exclaimed.

'Oh here we go again! Chandrani, how many times have I told you that there're no such things as ghosts,' said Arjun, with determination in his voice.

Chandrani ignored him and said, 'Many people have felt a presence in that house. There's actually a tragic incident behind it.'

'What incident?' asked Joy.

Chandrani looked at Arjun.

'Fine! You can tell the story. But, I'm sure Joy and Dipak don't believe in ghosts,' said Arjun.

'Hey that's for them to decide,' said Chandrani.

The mellow January sun had begun to set. A cool breeze blew over the field and rustled through the leaves of the trees as Chandrani embarked on her tale.

'A hundred years ago, that bungalow used to belong to an old businessman and his wife. Their only son was at odds with them. The parents did not approve of the woman their son had married. Hence, the feud. Eventually, the old man's wife died and he too became severely ill with a fatal disease. However, his son and daughter-in-law refused to take him in to live with them. They left him all alone and uncared for in that empty old house. By this time, the old man couldn't walk properly and had to use a walking stick. Every night, his sole pleasure was to walk through the corridors of his house and reminisce the events of his life. Finally, one morning, the caretaker of the house found him lying lifeless in one of the corridors. The old man's son and daughter-in-law were informed of his demise, but, they refused to come. Therefore, the last rites were performed by the village people. However, it is believed that his soul never attained eternal peace and continues to wander in his beloved bungalow.'

Chandrani finished her story. The daylight had disappeared. Another cold breeze blew over the field. It made the friends shiver.

'So that tapping sound…' said Dipak, swallowing hard in an attempt to get rid of the lump in his throat.

'That's the sound of the old man's walking stick,' said Chandrani.

Arjun let out a frustrated sigh. 'Oh come on, these things are just yarns spun by the village people!'

'No way,' protested Chandrani.

Dipak shuddered.

'It's getting cold out here. Let's go inside,' said Arjun.

The scholars got up to go indoors.

They found an empty classroom and went inside. In half an hour, the session would break for tea.

Chandrani turned towards Arjun and said, 'If it's proof you want, then why don't we all spend the night there?'

'This is ridiculous,' said Arjun.

'It's not. In fact, I *challenge* you to spend the night there...'

'Fine!'

'Fine'

'Not to interrupt or anything, but, I'm not sure that I want to spend another night in that house...' said Dipak.

'Ditto,' said Joy.

'Look, if it'll make you guys feel any better, y'all can stay at Arjun's place for the remainder of the conference. But, come with us tonight. It'll be fun,' insisted Chandrani.

Dipak and Joy looked at each other uneasily.

'Alright, we'll come,' said Joy, at last.

It was 10:30PM when the four arrived at the old bungalow. They walked down the corridor and into the room where their friends from Kolkata were staying. Dipak switched on the lights and closed the door.

What now?' demanded Arjun.

'Now, we wait,' said Chandrani.

'Wait all you want. But, I'm telling you, nothing's going to happen,' said Arjun, his voice overflowing with sarcasm.

The night was growing old. The tireless ticking of the clock was starting to take a toll on their patience. Dogs howled in the distance. A lizard crawled along the wall and hid itself behind a cupboard.

'Alright. Enough is enough! This is boring! Let's go home,' said Arjun, getting up from his chair.

Suddenly, the lights flickered, and almost simultaneously, the sound of footsteps was heard in the corridor. The tapping sound of the walking stick was also unmistakable. Tap. Tap. Tap.

'It's the old man,' whispered Chandrani.

'That's the sound that had kept us up for the past few nights,' said Dipak and Joy, in unison.

'It's him. He's here,' said Chandrani.

Without a word, Arjun ran to door, opened it and peered out into the corridor. A few minutes later, he closed the door and came back. 'This is impossible! There's no one there and yet the sound keeps coming,' he said.

'Then I guess this is proof enough, right?' said Chandrani.

'No way! This is an old house. Most of it is in ruins. Strange sounds are more than likely here. That doesn't mean that it's being caused by ghosts!'

Chandrani let out a frustrated sigh. 'You are one stubborn person!' she exclaimed angrily.

'I'm not stubborn! I'll believe it when I see it with my own eyes,' said Arjun.

All this time, Joy had been silently listening to the conversation that was going on between Chandrani and Arjun. He now decided to speak up.

'There is, however, one thing that we can do,' he said.

'What?' demanded Chandrani and Arjun.

'We can perform a séance and see if someone *is* indeed here,' said Joy.

'We don't know how to do that,' said Chandrani.

'I do,' said Joy.

Dipak, Chandrani and Arjun looked at him in astonishment.

'Yes, it's true. My mother was something of a medium herself. Growing up in her shadow, I know how to contact the spirit world,' said Arjun.

'Great! So, how do we do it?' asked Chandrani.

'Just do as I say,' said Joy, taking the lead.

The friends switched off the lights, lit a candle and sat holding hands in a circle around it.

'Close your eyes, and concentrate,' instructed Joy.

Everybody did as they were told. The room became steeped in complete silence. Joy cleared his throat and chanted, 'If there is anybody here who wants to make his or her presence felt, please respond to our call...'

He was met with silence. Even the sound of footsteps outside had ceased.

He chanted thus a few more times, until a strong gust of wind threw the windows open and blew out the candle.

The friends opened their eyes with a start. The room was submerged in darkness.

'This is a sign. There is undoubtedly a presence here,' observed Joy.

'There *is not*. There's nobody here,' protested Arjun.

'Fine. If that's the case, then let's try the same thing once more. Close the windows,' said Joy.

'I'll light the candle,' said Dipak, taking hold of the matchbox.

This time, however, the candle went out as soon as it was lit. The same thing happened three more times. The sound of footsteps resumed in the corridor. This time, it was louder than before.

'Look, there *is* someone in this house- a presence- who does not want to be disturbed. Out of respect for the departed, we should leave this place and go. *Now,*' said Joy, his voice sounding conclusive.

'But this makes no sense!' exclaimed Arjun.

'Well, sometimes, things don't make sense,' said Chandrani, in exasperation.

'Arjun, you have a scientific mind and that's praiseworthy. But, sometimes, you have to accept that there are things that cannot be explained logically and you *have* to be okay with that. Now grab your things and let's get out of here. Now,' said Joy.

'Fine,' said Arjun, giving in at last.

As the four gathered their belongings and stepped out of the house, the wind picked up

'It's getting really stormy,' observed Chandrani.

Arjun fetched inside his pockets and let out an expletive. 'I think I've left my phone inside the house. I'll be right back,' he said, as he ran back into the bungalow.

Fifteen minutes passed. The wind had ceased.

Chandrani swatted a mosquito with her hands. 'What is taking him so long?' she demanded, impatiently.

'Maybe I should go inside and help him,' said Dipak.

At that very moment, Arjun emerged out of the bungalow.

'There he is,' said Joy.

Arjun seemed visibly rattled. The others went over to him.

'Did you find your phone?' asked Dipak.

Arjun shook his head in the affirmative.

'What's wrong?' inquired Chandrani, anxiously.

'I saw him Chandrani...He's still there...' mumbled Arjun.

'Who's "he"?'

'The old businessman...I saw him...He was standing in the corridor...with his walking stick...staring at me. I saw him...with my own eyes...Then he disappeared...into thin air...'

None of them could believe their ears! A chill ran down their spines!

'Let's get out of here,' said Chandrani, leading the way.

The four sat in the living room of Arjun's place, sipping on cups of hot chocolate that Chandrani had made. The hot beverage helped to soothe their nerves.

'Thanks for letting us stay with you for the next couple of days, Arjun,' said Joy.

Arjun smiled feebly and gave him a friendly pat on the shoulder. He then turned towards his girlfriend. 'I'm sorry I didn't believe you, Chandrani. I really am. I was stubborn and hard-headed and I apologise for that,' he said, in a repentant voice.

Chandrani went and sat down next to him. 'It's okay,' she said, with a smile. 'You know, a researcher *should* have a scientific mind, but he should *also* have a touch of the poetic imagination in his soul. Basically, what I'm saying is that one should always keep one's heart and mind open to possibilities.'

'Listen to her, Arjun. She's a wise one you've got there,' said Joy.

Arjun looked into Chandrani's eyes. 'I promise I'll listen to you from now on. I promise that I'll believe in the endless possibilities of this universe,' he said.

'That's my big, strong man,' said Chandrani, with a smile.

Arjun laughed and pulled Chandrani into an embrace.

Dipak and Joy couldn't stop themselves from smiling.

ᏄᏄᏄ

Author Details

8
Sanchita Chakraborty

Sanchita Chakraborty is a teacher at K. E. Carmel School, Suri. She holds a Master's degree in English and Culture Studies from The University of Burdwan. Passionate about exploring life through words, Sanchita inspires all to appreciate the shades of language and literature.

9

Dr Debosree Ghosh

Dr. Debosree Ghosh is an Assistant Professor in the Department of Physiology, Government General Degree College, Kharagpur II, West Bengal, India. Dr. Ghosh has been awarded Gold Medal by the University of Calcutta for holding 1st rank in M.Sc. in Human Physiology and received DST INSPIRE Fellowship in 2011 from the Ministry of Science, India, to pursue her Ph.D. in Physiology from the University of Calcutta. She has been awarded the Dr. D.N. Mullick Memorial Prize of the Physiological Society of India. She received a travel grant from the University of Calcutta for presenting her research work at the South Asian Association of Physiologists Conference, held in Colombo, Srilanka. She has been awarded a certificate of merit for the XXVI Training Programme on Science Communication and Media Practice held under the aegis of the Indian Science News Association. She has published more than 90 articles in peer-reviewed national and international journals. She has authored several book chapters in books published by national and international publishers. She has published more than 43 popular science articles in several newsletters. She has authored her first short story "An Unusual Winter Tale" in the anthology 'Winter Musings' published by Rhythmic Publishers. She is on the editorial board and serves as a reviewer in several national and international journals. She has delivered lectures at several national and international conferences in India and abroad.

10
Mala Bhattacharya

Mala Bhattacharya grew up with love for Literature in the beautiful Steel Township, Jamshedpur. Having completed her English Lit (Hons), she went on to complete her M.A. in English Literature. Shifting to Bombay post marriage, she entered the teaching arena as a teacher and HOD of English in various schools. Meanwhile, she obtained her B.ed degree with a First Class from Bombay

University. Her principalship stint soon saw her helming Sir J.J. Girls' High School, one of the oldest and prestigious institutions run by the benevolent and illustrious Jeejeebhoy family. Her second post - graduate degree in Education, M.A. (Ed) securing again a First Class ensured her smooth transition to the IGCSE (Cambridge) Boards, opted by 'National Education School'. At present after retirement, she continues, to tutor and mentor pupils online of different Indian as well as Cambridge Boards alongwith her other pursuits in Kolkata.

11

Mandira Ghosh

Mandira Ghosh is a maths educator by profession and a writer by passion. She works as a maths trainer at Bhanzu, an edtech company, and hails from Suri, Birbhum, West Bengal. She writes poems, creative prose, and short stories. She explores and tries to give voice to her logical and imaginative thoughts in her work.

55

12

Dr Debasri Mukherjee

I was born and grew up in a joint family in Kolkata, West Bengal, India. At that time everyone knew it as Calcutta.My schooling was at Loreto Convent. I went on to do my Bachelors and Masters in Human Physiology from the University of Calcutta. Then I did my Ph.D in Cardiovascular Physiology also from the Dept. of Physiology, University of Calcutta, under the supervision of Prof Debasish Bandyopadhyay.I did my post-doctoral research in immune-cell biology and proteomics from the National Centre for Cell Science of the Dept. of Biotechnology, GOI, in Pune, Maharashtra, India. Then I joined Cactus Communications Pvt Ltd as a Scientific Writer.I am passionate about writing and have dabbled in multiple genres of fiction writing, from ghost stories to children's tales. Other than that, I enjoy swimming, traveling, and reading story books.My family comprises my parents, my aunt and uncle, my mother-in-law, my husband, and our black Labrador named Nemo (from Jules Verne's Captain Nemo. Not the fish).

13

Dr Sukanya Bhattacharya

Dr. Sukanya Bhattacharya is an Associate Professor in the Department of Botany, Vidyasagar College, Kolkata. Dr. Bhattacharya has a brilliant academic profile with high First class in both B.Sc and M.Sc exams of Calcutta

University. She had been a National Scholar and had the distinction of being a Direct Fellow CSIR, New Delhi. She obtained her Ph.D from Jadavpur University and since then had been a member of several learned bodies in India such as Life member Indian Science Congress Association, Life member Eastern India Horticulture and Biotechnology Centre. She has delivered several lectures at a number of symposia, seminars and conferences in India. She has several original research papers published in National and International journals of repute.

14

Aishi Bandyopadhyay

Ms. Aishi Bandyopadhyay has done her schooling from La Martiniere for Girls, Kolkata, graduated with Honours in English from Lady Brabourne College, Kolkata, affiliated under the University of Calcutta, and has completed her post-graduation in English Language and Literature from Presidency University, Kolkata. She has also completed a post-graduate certificate course in Editing and Publishing from the School of Cultural Texts and Records, Jadavpur

University and has founded her own publishing house, *Rhythmic Publishers*, in 2023. She is an ardent lover of music and a student of Rabindrasangeet. In her leisure hours, she loves listening to music, read books (especially detective fiction and ghost stories) and paint. She also enjoys photography. An animal-lover and an admirer of nature, she enjoys travelling to the seaside and to historical places. An introvert by nature, it gives her immense pleasure to spend some quiet time at home with her family.

Aishi is a widely acclaimed author. Her books *Chills and Thrills* and *Shadows & Suspense* have received praise and appreciation from readers across the globe.Her book, *Shadows and Suspense,* had also been nominated for a Popular Choice Award in the 6th Season of "AutHer Awards", 2025, organized jointly by JK Paper and The Times of India. Several of her short stories have been published in anthologies.